Addition Facts 1-6

The answer to an addition problem is called the **sum**.
You can write an **addition number sentence** like this: **2 + 3 = 5**

$$\underline{2} + \underline{3} = \underline{5}$$

Write a **number sentence** about the pictures.

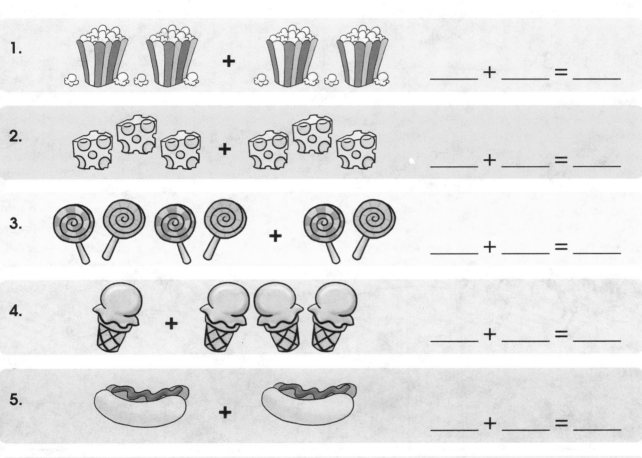

1. ____ + ____ = ____

2. ____ + ____ = ____

3. ____ + ____ = ____

4. ____ + ____ = ____

5. ____ + ____ = ____

6. ____ + ____ = ____

7.

1

You can use a number line to find the **sum** for **4 + 2**.
Start at **4**. Then count on **2** more numbers: **4**, ...**5**, **6**.

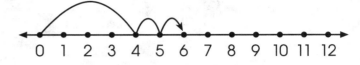

$$4 + 2 = 6 \qquad 4 + 2 = 6$$

Find the **sum**. Use the number line if you need help.

1. $3 + 3 = \underline{\qquad}$ 2. $1 + 4 = \underline{\qquad}$ 3. $4 + 2 = \underline{\qquad}$

4. $5 + 1 = \underline{\qquad}$ 5. $2 + 3 = \underline{\qquad}$ 6. $2 + 2 = \underline{\qquad}$

7. $\begin{array}{r} 4 \\ +\ 1 \\ \hline \end{array}$ 8. $\begin{array}{r} 2 \\ +\ 4 \\ \hline \end{array}$ 9. $\begin{array}{r} 3 \\ +\ 3 \\ \hline \end{array}$ 10. $\begin{array}{r} 1 \\ +\ 1 \\ \hline \end{array}$ 11. $\begin{array}{r} 1 \\ +\ 5 \\ \hline \end{array}$

12. $\begin{array}{r} 2 \\ +\ 2 \\ \hline \end{array}$ 13. $\begin{array}{r} 1 \\ +\ 2 \\ \hline \end{array}$ 14. $\begin{array}{r} 4 \\ +\ 2 \\ \hline \end{array}$ 15. $\begin{array}{r} 3 \\ +\ 2 \\ \hline \end{array}$ 16. $\begin{array}{r} 1 \\ +\ 3 \\ \hline \end{array}$

The answer to a subtraction problem is called the **difference**.
You can write a **subtraction number sentence** like this: **4 – 2 = 2**

Write a **number sentence** about the pictures.

1.    _____ – _____ = _____

2.    _____ – _____ = _____

3.    _____ – _____ = _____

4.    _____ – _____ = _____

5.    _____ – _____ = _____

6.    _____ – _____ = _____

7.    _____ – _____ = _____

You can use a number line to find the **difference** for **5 – 2**.
Start at **5**. Then count back **2** numbers: **5, ...4, 3**.

The **difference** of **5 – 2** is **3**.

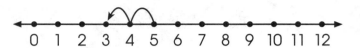

$$5 - 2 = 3$$

Find the **difference**. Use the number line if you need help.

1. $6 - 3 =$ _____   2. $5 - 2 =$ _____   3. $4 - 2 =$ _____

4. $3 - 2 =$ _____   5. $3 - 1 =$ _____   6. $2 - 1 =$ _____

7. $\begin{array}{r} 5 \\ -1 \\ \hline \end{array}$ 8. $\begin{array}{r} 6 \\ -4 \\ \hline \end{array}$ 9. $\begin{array}{r} 5 \\ -3 \\ \hline \end{array}$ 10. $\begin{array}{r} 6 \\ -1 \\ \hline \end{array}$

11. $\begin{array}{r} 5 \\ -4 \\ \hline \end{array}$ 12. $\begin{array}{r} 4 \\ -2 \\ \hline \end{array}$ 13. $\begin{array}{r} 6 \\ -3 \\ \hline \end{array}$ 14. $\begin{array}{r} 6 \\ -5 \\ \hline \end{array}$

15. $\begin{array}{r} 5 \\ -2 \\ \hline \end{array}$ 16. $\begin{array}{r} 4 \\ -3 \\ \hline \end{array}$ 17. $\begin{array}{r} 3 \\ -2 \\ \hline \end{array}$ 18. $\begin{array}{r} 6 \\ -2 \\ \hline \end{array}$

```
0+0=0                    0-0=0
1+0=1        0+1=1       1-0=1        1-1=0
2+0=2        1+1=2       2-0=2        2-1=1
3+0=3        2+1=3       3-0=3        3-1=2
4+0=4        3+1=4       4-0=4        4-1=3
5+0=5        4+1=5       5-0=5        5-1=4
6+0=6        5+1=6       6-0=6        6-1=5
```

Find the **sum**.

1.   4
   + 0

2.   2
   + 1

3.   5
   + 1

4.   1
   + 4

5.   2
   + 0

6.   1
   + 1

7.   5
   + 0

8.   0
   + 1

9.   1
   + 3

10.   6
    + 0

Find the **difference**.

11.   3
    − 1

12.   2
    − 1

13.   4
    − 1

14.   3
    − 0

15.   1
    − 1

16.   5
    − 0

17.   6
    − 1

18.   0
    − 0

19.   2
    − 0

20.   4
    − 0

Adding and Subtracting 0 and 1

A **fact family** uses the same numbers in its addition and subtraction number sentences.

One fact family of **5** uses the numbers **2**, **3**, and **5**.

Other fact families for **5** might use the numbers **1**, **4**, and **5** or **0**, **5**, and **5**.

2 + 3 = 5	1 + 4 = 5	0 + 5 = 5
3 + 2 = 5	4 + 1 = 5	5 + 0 = 5
5 − 2 = 3	5 − 1 = 4	5 − 0 = 5
5 − 3 = 2	5 − 4 = 1	5 − 5 = 0

Find the **sum(s)** and **difference(s)** for the **fact family**.

1.
$$1 + 3 \qquad 3 + 1 \qquad 4 - 1 \qquad 4 - 3$$

2.
$$5 + 1 \qquad 1 + 5 \qquad 6 - 5 \qquad 6 - 1$$

3.
$$4 + 0 \qquad 0 + 4 \qquad 4 - 4 \qquad 4 - 0$$

4.
$$3 + 3 \qquad 6 - 3$$

5.
$$3 + 3 \qquad 6 - 3$$

6.
$$2 + 2 \qquad 4 - 2$$

Write the **sums** or **differences**.

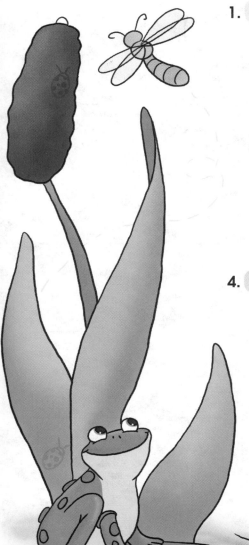

1. Add **1**

4 _5_

2 ___

0 ___

5 ___

2. Add **3**

1 ___

3 ___

2 ___

0 ___

3. Add **0**

6 ___

4 ___

1 ___

5 ___

4. Subtract **1**

6 _5_

3 ___

5 ___

2 ___

5. Subtract **0**

5 ___

2 ___

6 ___

1 ___

6. Subtract **2**

2 ___

3 ___

6 ___

5 ___

7. How many hidden s can you find in the picture? Finish the puzzle to find the answer.

| 2 | +4 | | −3 | | −1 | | +2 | = | | s |

Adding and Subtracting 0–6

$$\underline{5} + \underline{2} = \underline{7}$$

Write a **number sentence** about the pictures.

1. _____ + _____ = _____

2. _____ + _____ = _____

3. _____ + _____ = _____

4. _____ + _____ = _____

5. _____ + _____ = _____

6. _____ + _____ = _____

7. _____ + _____ = _____

8

$$\underline{7} - \underline{3} = \underline{4}$$

Write a **number sentence** about the pictures.

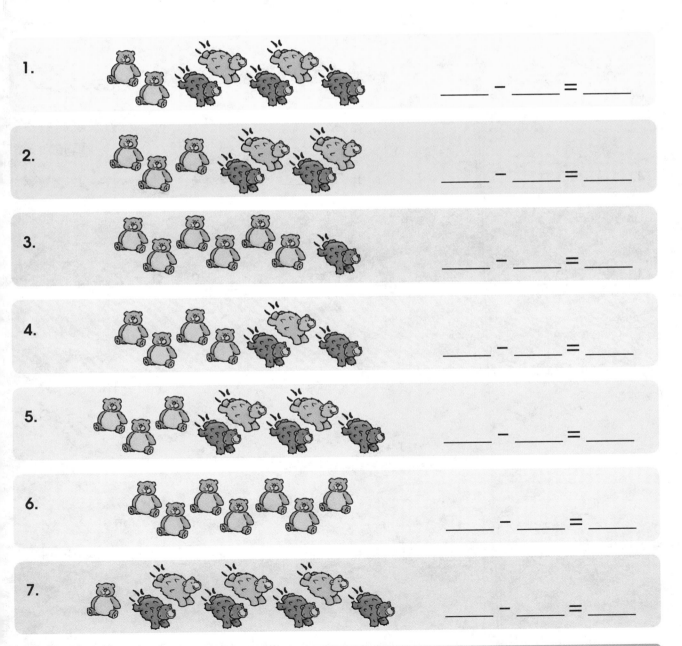

1. _____ - _____ = _____

2. _____ - _____ = _____

3. _____ - _____ = _____

4. _____ - _____ = _____

5. _____ - _____ = _____

6. _____ - _____ = _____

7. _____ - _____ = _____

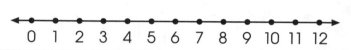

0 1 2 3 4 5 6 7 8 9 10 11 12

Find the **sum** or **difference**. Use the number line if you need help.

1. $4 + 3 =$ _____

2. $6 + 2 =$ _____

3. $8 - 4 =$ _____

4. $8 - 3 =$ _____

5. $1 + 6 =$ _____

6. $7 - 4 =$ _____

7. $2 + 5 =$ _____

8. $7 + 1 =$ _____

9. $8 - 2 =$ _____

10.
$$\begin{array}{r} 6 \\ +\ 2 \\ \hline \end{array}$$

11.
$$\begin{array}{r} 7 \\ -\ 2 \\ \hline \end{array}$$

12.
$$\begin{array}{r} 0 \\ +\ 7 \\ \hline \end{array}$$

13.
$$\begin{array}{r} 8 \\ -\ 2 \\ \hline \end{array}$$

14.
$$\begin{array}{r} 8 \\ -\ 5 \\ \hline \end{array}$$

15.
$$\begin{array}{r} 7 \\ -\ 5 \\ \hline \end{array}$$

16.
$$\begin{array}{r} 8 \\ -\ 3 \\ \hline \end{array}$$

17.
$$\begin{array}{r} 5 \\ +\ 3 \\ \hline \end{array}$$

18.
$$\begin{array}{r} 7 \\ -\ 3 \\ \hline \end{array}$$

19.
$$\begin{array}{r} 4 \\ +\ 4 \\ \hline \end{array}$$

Here is a **fact family** for **8**.
It uses the numbers **3**, **5**, and **8**.

 $3 + 5 = 8$ $5 + 3 = 8$ $8 - 3 = 5$ $8 - 5 = 3$

Find the **sum(s)** and **difference(s)** for the **fact family**.

1.
$\begin{array}{r} 4 \\ + 3 \\ \hline \end{array}$
$\begin{array}{r} 3 \\ + 4 \\ \hline \end{array}$
$\begin{array}{r} 7 \\ - 4 \\ \hline \end{array}$
$\begin{array}{r} 7 \\ - 3 \\ \hline \end{array}$

2.
$\begin{array}{r} 4 \\ + 4 \\ \hline \end{array}$
$\begin{array}{r} 8 \\ - 4 \\ \hline \end{array}$

3.
$\begin{array}{r} 2 \\ + 5 \\ \hline \end{array}$
$\begin{array}{r} 5 \\ + 2 \\ \hline \end{array}$
$\begin{array}{r} 7 \\ - 2 \\ \hline \end{array}$
$\begin{array}{r} 7 \\ - 5 \\ \hline \end{array}$

4.
$\begin{array}{r} 2 \\ + 6 \\ \hline \end{array}$
$\begin{array}{r} 6 \\ + 2 \\ \hline \end{array}$
$\begin{array}{r} 8 \\ - 2 \\ \hline \end{array}$
$\begin{array}{r} 8 \\ - 6 \\ \hline \end{array}$

5.
$\begin{array}{r} 7 \\ + 1 \\ \hline \end{array}$
$\begin{array}{r} 1 \\ + 7 \\ \hline \end{array}$
$\begin{array}{r} 8 \\ - 7 \\ \hline \end{array}$
$\begin{array}{r} 8 \\ - 1 \\ \hline \end{array}$

6.
$\begin{array}{r} 0 \\ + 8 \\ \hline \end{array}$
$\begin{array}{r} 8 \\ - 8 \\ \hline \end{array}$

$\underline{3} + \underline{6} = \underline{9}$

Write a **number sentence** about the pictures.

1. ____ + ____ = ____

2. ____ + ____ = ____

3. ____ + ____ = ____

4. ____ + ____ = ____

5. ____ + ____ = ____

6. ____ + ____ = ____

7. ____ + ____ = ____

$$10 - 6 = 4$$

Write a **number sentence** about the pictures.

1.  _____ – _____ = _____

2.  _____ – _____ = _____

3.  _____ – _____ = _____

4.  _____ – _____ = _____

5.  _____ – _____ = _____

6.  _____ – _____ = _____

7.  _____ – _____ = _____

Subtraction Facts 9 and 10

Here is a **fact family** for **9**.
It uses the numbers **1**, **8**, and **9**.

$$
\begin{array}{r} 1 \\ + 8 \\ \hline 9 \end{array}
\qquad
\begin{array}{r} 8 \\ + 1 \\ \hline 9 \end{array}
\qquad
\begin{array}{r} 9 \\ - 1 \\ \hline 8 \end{array}
\qquad
\begin{array}{r} 9 \\ - 8 \\ \hline 1 \end{array}
$$

Find the **sum(s)** and **difference(s)** for the **fact family**.

1.
$$
\begin{array}{r} 6 \\ + 3 \\ \hline \end{array}
\qquad
\begin{array}{r} 3 \\ + 6 \\ \hline \end{array}
\qquad
\begin{array}{r} 9 \\ - 6 \\ \hline \end{array}
\qquad
\begin{array}{r} 9 \\ - 3 \\ \hline \end{array}
$$

2.
$$
\begin{array}{r} 5 \\ + 4 \\ \hline \end{array}
\qquad
\begin{array}{r} 4 \\ + 5 \\ \hline \end{array}
\qquad
\begin{array}{r} 9 \\ - 5 \\ \hline \end{array}
\qquad
\begin{array}{r} 9 \\ - 4 \\ \hline \end{array}
$$

3.
$$
\begin{array}{r} 6 \\ + 4 \\ \hline \end{array}
\qquad
\begin{array}{r} 4 \\ + 6 \\ \hline \end{array}
\qquad
\begin{array}{r} 10 \\ - 6 \\ \hline \end{array}
\qquad
\begin{array}{r} 10 \\ - 4 \\ \hline \end{array}
$$

4.
$$
\begin{array}{r} 7 \\ + 3 \\ \hline \end{array}
\qquad
\begin{array}{r} 3 \\ + 7 \\ \hline \end{array}
\qquad
\begin{array}{r} 10 \\ - 7 \\ \hline \end{array}
\qquad
\begin{array}{r} 10 \\ - 3 \\ \hline \end{array}
$$

5.
$$
\begin{array}{r} 2 \\ + 8 \\ \hline \end{array}
\qquad
\begin{array}{r} 8 \\ + 2 \\ \hline \end{array}
\qquad
\begin{array}{r} 10 \\ - 2 \\ \hline \end{array}
\qquad
\begin{array}{r} 10 \\ - 8 \\ \hline \end{array}
$$

6.
$$
\begin{array}{r} 10 \\ - 5 \\ \hline \end{array}
\qquad
\begin{array}{r} 5 \\ + 5 \\ \hline \end{array}
$$

Find the **sum** or **difference**. Use the number line if you need help.

1. $9 - 3 =$ _____
2. $4 + 5 =$ _____
3. $9 - 4 =$ _____

4. $5 + 5 =$ _____
5. $9 - 7 =$ _____
6. $10 - 2 =$ _____

7. $4 + 6 =$ _____
8. $10 - 4 =$ _____
9. $7 + 2 =$ _____

10.
$$\begin{array}{r} 7 \\ + 3 \\ \hline \end{array}$$

11.
$$\begin{array}{r} 8 \\ + 2 \\ \hline \end{array}$$

12.
$$\begin{array}{r} 9 \\ - 0 \\ \hline \end{array}$$

13.
$$\begin{array}{r} 9 \\ - 6 \\ \hline \end{array}$$

14.
$$\begin{array}{r} 9 \\ - 2 \\ \hline \end{array}$$

15.
$$\begin{array}{r} 3 \\ + 7 \\ \hline \end{array}$$

16.
$$\begin{array}{r} 6 \\ + 4 \\ \hline \end{array}$$

17.
$$\begin{array}{r} 10 \\ - 5 \\ \hline \end{array}$$

18.
$$\begin{array}{r} 9 \\ - 1 \\ \hline \end{array}$$

Addition and Subtraction Facts 9 and 10

Find the **sum** or **difference**. Be careful!

1. $9 - 3 =$ ____
2. $10 - 7 =$ ____

3. $6 + 4 =$ ____
4. $2 + 8 =$ ____

5. $5 + 3 =$ ____
6. $10 - 2 =$ ____

7. $8 - 5 =$ ____
8. $5 + 4 =$ ____

9.
$$\begin{array}{r} 0 \\ + 4 \\ \hline \end{array}$$
10.
$$\begin{array}{r} 6 \\ + 3 \\ \hline \end{array}$$
11.
$$\begin{array}{r} 9 \\ - 6 \\ \hline \end{array}$$

12.
$$\begin{array}{r} 9 \\ - 2 \\ \hline \end{array}$$
13.
$$\begin{array}{r} 9 \\ - 3 \\ \hline \end{array}$$
14.
$$\begin{array}{r} 5 \\ + 2 \\ \hline \end{array}$$

15.
$$\begin{array}{r} 3 \\ + 4 \\ \hline \end{array}$$
16.
$$\begin{array}{r} 10 \\ - 8 \\ \hline \end{array}$$
17.
$$\begin{array}{r} 4 \\ + 4 \\ \hline \end{array}$$

18.
$$\begin{array}{r} 7 \\ + 3 \\ \hline \end{array}$$
19.
$$\begin{array}{r} 6 \\ - 0 \\ \hline \end{array}$$
20.
$$\begin{array}{r} 7 \\ + 2 \\ \hline \end{array}$$

Addition and Subtraction Facts 0–10
©School Zone Publishing Company

Look at the problem. What's missing?
The problem needs a **+** or **–** sign.
Write **+** or **–** in the box to make the problem true.

$$\boxed{+}\ \begin{array}{r} 6 \\ 3 \\ \hline 9 \end{array}$$

$$\boxed{-}\ \begin{array}{r} 7 \\ 3 \\ \hline 4 \end{array}$$

1. $$\square\ \begin{array}{r} 5 \\ 5 \\ \hline 10 \end{array}$$

2. $$\square\ \begin{array}{r} 6 \\ 2 \\ \hline 4 \end{array}$$

3. $$\square\ \begin{array}{r} 5 \\ 3 \\ \hline 2 \end{array}$$

4. $$\square\ \begin{array}{r} 8 \\ 2 \\ \hline 10 \end{array}$$

5. $$\square\ \begin{array}{r} 8 \\ 5 \\ \hline 3 \end{array}$$

6. $$\square\ \begin{array}{r} 2 \\ 6 \\ \hline 8 \end{array}$$

7. $$\square\ \begin{array}{r} 6 \\ 4 \\ \hline 2 \end{array}$$

8. $$\square\ \begin{array}{r} 7 \\ 1 \\ \hline 6 \end{array}$$

9. $$\square\ \begin{array}{r} 6 \\ 3 \\ \hline 9 \end{array}$$

10. $$\square\ \begin{array}{r} 9 \\ 4 \\ \hline 5 \end{array}$$

11. $$\square\ \begin{array}{r} 8 \\ 6 \\ \hline 2 \end{array}$$

12. $$\square\ \begin{array}{r} 2 \\ 5 \\ \hline 7 \end{array}$$

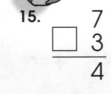

13. $$\square\ \begin{array}{r} 2 \\ 6 \\ \hline 8 \end{array}$$

14. $$\square\ \begin{array}{r} 9 \\ 5 \\ \hline 4 \end{array}$$

15. $$\square\ \begin{array}{r} 7 \\ 3 \\ \hline 4 \end{array}$$

16. $$\square\ \begin{array}{r} 4 \\ 6 \\ \hline 10 \end{array}$$

Addition and Subtraction Facts 1–10

$$8 + 4 = 12$$

Write a **number sentence** about the pictures.

1. _____ + _____ = _____

2. _____ + _____ = _____

3. _____ + _____ = _____

4. _____ + _____ = _____

5. _____ + _____ = _____

6. _____ + _____ = _____

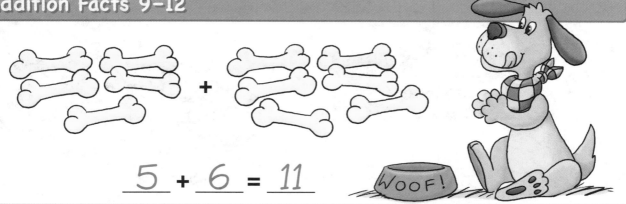

$$\underline{5} + \underline{6} = \underline{11}$$

Find the **sum**.

1. $8 + 3 = $ ____

2. $5 + 7 = $ ____

3. $6 + 4 = $ ____

4. $9 + 2 = $ ____

5. $1 + 8 = $ ____

6. $7 + 2 = $ ____

7. $5 + 6 = $ ____

8. $9 + 0 = $ ____

9. $5 + 5 = $ ____

10.
$$\begin{array}{r} 9 \\ + 3 \\ \hline \end{array}$$

11.
$$\begin{array}{r} 2 \\ + 8 \\ \hline \end{array}$$

12.
$$\begin{array}{r} 7 \\ + 4 \\ \hline \end{array}$$

13.
$$\begin{array}{r} 6 \\ + 6 \\ \hline \end{array}$$

14.
$$\begin{array}{r} 8 \\ + 4 \\ \hline \end{array}$$

15.
$$\begin{array}{r} 9 \\ + 1 \\ \hline \end{array}$$

16.
$$\begin{array}{r} 4 \\ + 5 \\ \hline \end{array}$$

17.
$$\begin{array}{r} 7 \\ + 3 \\ \hline \end{array}$$

18.
$$\begin{array}{r} 8 \\ + 2 \\ \hline \end{array}$$

19.
$$\begin{array}{r} 7 \\ + 5 \\ \hline \end{array}$$

20.
$$\begin{array}{r} 6 \\ + 3 \\ \hline \end{array}$$

21.
$$\begin{array}{r} 4 \\ + 7 \\ \hline \end{array}$$

$$\underline{11} - \underline{4} = \underline{7}$$

Write a **number sentence** about the pictures.

1.    _____ – _____ = _____

2.    _____ – _____ = _____

3.    _____ – _____ = _____

4.    _____ – _____ = _____

5.    _____ – _____ = _____

6.    _____ – _____ = _____

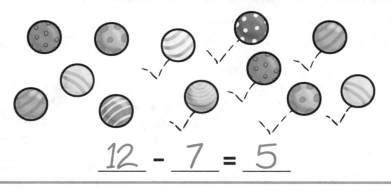

$$\underline{12} - \underline{7} = \underline{5}$$

Find the **difference**.

1. $11 - 3 = \underline{\hphantom{000}}$ 2. $12 - 9 = \underline{\hphantom{000}}$ 3. $11 - 7 = \underline{\hphantom{000}}$

4. $12 - 4 = \underline{\hphantom{000}}$ 5. $10 - 5 = \underline{\hphantom{000}}$ 6. $11 - 2 = \underline{\hphantom{000}}$

7. $10 - 7 = \underline{\hphantom{000}}$ 8. $12 - 8 = \underline{\hphantom{000}}$ 9. $12 - 3 = \underline{\hphantom{000}}$

10. $\begin{array}{r} 12 \\ -\ 9 \\ \hline \end{array}$ 11. $\begin{array}{r} 11 \\ -\ 5 \\ \hline \end{array}$ 12. $\begin{array}{r} 9 \\ -\ 7 \\ \hline \end{array}$ 13. $\begin{array}{r} 10 \\ -\ 9 \\ \hline \end{array}$

14. $\begin{array}{r} 11 \\ -\ 4 \\ \hline \end{array}$ 15. $\begin{array}{r} 12 \\ -\ 7 \\ \hline \end{array}$ 16. $\begin{array}{r} 11 \\ -\ 8 \\ \hline \end{array}$ 17. $\begin{array}{r} 10 \\ -\ 4 \\ \hline \end{array}$

18. $\begin{array}{r} 9 \\ -\ 6 \\ \hline \end{array}$ 19. $\begin{array}{r} 11 \\ -\ 6 \\ \hline \end{array}$ 20. $\begin{array}{r} 12 \\ -\ 5 \\ \hline \end{array}$ 21. $\begin{array}{r} 12 \\ -\ 3 \\ \hline \end{array}$

Find the **sum(s)** and **difference(s)** for the **fact family**. Use the number line if you need help.

1.
```
  2      9     11     11
+ 9    + 2    - 2    - 9
```

2.
```
  6     12
+ 6    - 6
```

3.
```
  4      8     12     12
+ 8    + 4    - 4    - 8
```

4.
```
  5      6     11     11
+ 6    + 5    - 5    - 6
```

5.
```
  4      7     11     11
+ 7    + 4    - 4    - 7
```

6.
```
  3      8     11     11
+ 8    + 3    - 3    - 8
```

7.
```
  9      3     12     12
+ 3    + 9    - 9    - 3
```

8.
```
  5      7     12     12
+ 7    + 5    - 5    - 7
```

Find each **sum** and **difference**.
Circle the clown with the greatest answer.

1.	2.	3.	4.	5.	6.
9	4	12	0	7	5
+ 3	+ 7	− 8	+ 9	− 3	+ 2
− 6	− 6	− 4	+ 2	+ 8	− 4
− 3	+ 5	+ 5	− 7	− 4	− 2
=	=	=	=	=	=

Addition and Subtraction Facts 0-12

The numbers you add are called **addends**.
You can add three numbers in different ways.

Add the numbers in order:
Add the first two numbers.
$4 + 2 = 6$

$$\begin{matrix} 4 \\ 2 \\ +\,6 \\ \hline 12 \end{matrix}$$

$4 + 2 = 6$

Then add the third number.
$6 + 6 = 12$

Look for a ten:
Look for two numbers with the sum of **10**.
$4 + 6 = 10$

$$\begin{matrix} 4 \\ 2 \\ +\,6 \\ \hline 12 \end{matrix}$$

$4 + 6 = 10$

Then add the third number.
$10 + 2 = 12$

Find the **sums**.

1.
$$\begin{matrix} 2 \\ 6 \\ +\,3 \\ \hline \end{matrix}$$

2.
$$\begin{matrix} 1 \\ 8 \\ +\,3 \\ \hline \end{matrix}$$

3.
$$\begin{matrix} 9 \\ 1 \\ +\,2 \\ \hline \end{matrix}$$

4.
$$\begin{matrix} 2 \\ 4 \\ +\,5 \\ \hline \end{matrix}$$

5.
$$\begin{matrix} 4 \\ 7 \\ +\,1 \\ \hline \end{matrix}$$

6.
$$\begin{matrix} 4 \\ 4 \\ +\,2 \\ \hline \end{matrix}$$

7.
$$\begin{matrix} 3 \\ 1 \\ +\,7 \\ \hline \end{matrix}$$

8.
$$\begin{matrix} 5 \\ 5 \\ +\,2 \\ \hline \end{matrix}$$

9.
$$\begin{matrix} 6 \\ 2 \\ +\,2 \\ \hline \end{matrix}$$

10.
$$\begin{matrix} 4 \\ 4 \\ +\,4 \\ \hline \end{matrix}$$

11.
$$\begin{matrix} 3 \\ 2 \\ +\,5 \\ \hline \end{matrix}$$

12.
$$\begin{matrix} 1 \\ 2 \\ +\,8 \\ \hline \end{matrix}$$

Three Addends; Sums to 12

Break the Code!

Find each **sum** and **difference**.
Use the code below to solve the riddle.

Riddle:
They are sometimes called "kings."
At the circus, they jump through rings.

1.	2.	3.	4.	5.
8	10	3	2	7
+ 2	− 5	+ 8	+ 6	− 4
− 8	+ 2	− 6	+ 3	+ 9
+ 7	+ 5	− 5	− 4	− 8
=	=	=	=	=

____   ____   ____   ____   ____

code

0	1	2	3	4	5	6	7	8	9	10	11	12
O	Z	E	B	S	R	K	N	H	L	F	P	I

Addition and Subtraction Facts 0–12

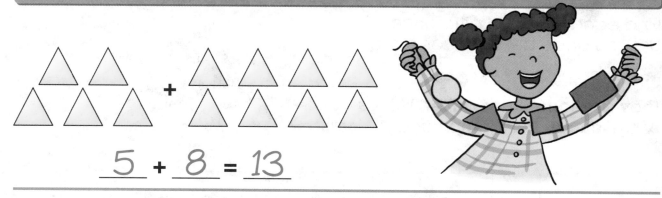

$$\underline{5} + \underline{8} = \underline{13}$$

Write a **number sentence** about the pictures.

1. ___ + ___ = ___

2. ___ + ___ = ___

3. ___ + ___ = ___

4. ___ + ___ = ___

5. ___ + ___ = ___

6. ___ + ___ = ___

Addend Turnaround

If you change the order of the **addends**, the **sum** is still the same.

$$5 + 4 = 9$$
$$4 + 5 = 9$$

Find the **sum**.

1. $5 + 6 = \underline{\hspace{1cm}}$ 　2. $6 + 5 = \underline{\hspace{1cm}}$ 　3. $6 + 8 = \underline{\hspace{1cm}}$ 　4. $8 + 6 = \underline{\hspace{1cm}}$

5. $4 + 7 = \underline{\hspace{1cm}}$ 　6. $7 + 4 = \underline{\hspace{1cm}}$ 　7. $8 + 2 = \underline{\hspace{1cm}}$ 　8. $2 + 8 = \underline{\hspace{1cm}}$

9. $8 + 5 = \underline{\hspace{1cm}}$ 　10. $5 + 8 = \underline{\hspace{1cm}}$ 　11. $4 + 9 = \underline{\hspace{1cm}}$ 　12. $9 + 4 = \underline{\hspace{1cm}}$

13. $7 + 3 = \underline{\hspace{1cm}}$ 　14. $3 + 7 = \underline{\hspace{1cm}}$ 　15. $7 + 5 = \underline{\hspace{1cm}}$ 　16. $5 + 7 = \underline{\hspace{1cm}}$

17. $6 + 7 = \underline{\hspace{1cm}}$ 　18. $7 + 6 = \underline{\hspace{1cm}}$ 　19. $5 + 9 = \underline{\hspace{1cm}}$ 　20. $9 + 5 = \underline{\hspace{1cm}}$

21. $4 + 8 = \underline{\hspace{1cm}}$ 　22. $8 + 4 = \underline{\hspace{1cm}}$ 　23. $3 + 8 = \underline{\hspace{1cm}}$ 　24. $8 + 3 = \underline{\hspace{1cm}}$

25. $9 + 3 = \underline{\hspace{1cm}}$ 　26. $3 + 9 = \underline{\hspace{1cm}}$ 　27. $7 + 2 = \underline{\hspace{1cm}}$ 　28. $2 + 7 = \underline{\hspace{1cm}}$

Order Property; Sums 9–14

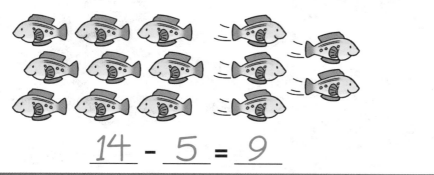 

$$14 - 5 = 9$$

Write a **number sentence** about the pictures.

1. _____ - _____ = _____

2. _____ - _____ = _____

3. _____ - _____ = _____

4.  _____ - _____ = _____

5.  _____ - _____ = _____

6.  _____ - _____ = _____

Which Number Is Missing?

Find the **missing number** in the problem.
Remember the addition and subtraction facts.

1. $7 + 5 = \boxed{}$

2. $14 - 7 = \boxed{}$

3. $12 - \boxed{} = 7$

4. $14 - 8 = \boxed{}$

5. $5 + \boxed{} = 13$

6. $5 + 9 = \boxed{}$

7. $8 + \boxed{} = 12$

8. $4 + 9 = \boxed{}$

9. $14 - 9 = \boxed{}$

10.
$$\begin{array}{r} 8 \\ + 3 \\ \hline \boxed{} \end{array}$$

11.
$$\begin{array}{r} 5 \\ + \boxed{} \\ \hline 13 \end{array}$$

12.
$$\begin{array}{r} 3 \\ + 9 \\ \hline \boxed{} \end{array}$$

13.
$$\begin{array}{r} 12 \\ - \boxed{} \\ \hline 4 \end{array}$$

14.
$$\begin{array}{r} 11 \\ - 7 \\ \hline \boxed{} \end{array}$$

15.
$$\begin{array}{r} 13 \\ - 5 \\ \hline \boxed{} \end{array}$$

16.
$$\begin{array}{r} 5 \\ + \boxed{} \\ \hline 11 \end{array}$$

17.
$$\begin{array}{r} 7 \\ + 5 \\ \hline \boxed{} \end{array}$$

18.
$$\begin{array}{r} 4 \\ + \boxed{} \\ \hline 12 \end{array}$$

19.
$$\begin{array}{r} 11 \\ - 3 \\ \hline \boxed{} \end{array}$$

Finding the Missing Numbers (Sums 11–14)

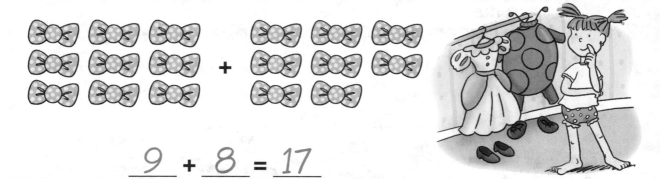

$$\underline{9} + \underline{8} = \underline{17}$$

Write a **number sentence** about the pictures.

1.

_____ + _____ = _____

2.

_____ + _____ = _____

3.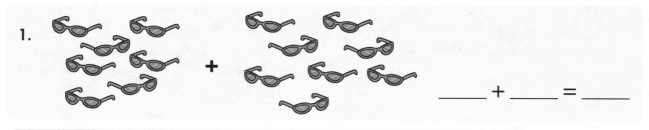

_____ + _____ = _____

4.

_____ + _____ = _____

5.

_____ + _____ = _____

Circle the pair(s) of **addends** that match the **sum**.

1.

10
5 + 5
4 + 6
3 + 8
5 + 4

2.

11
5 + 6
3 + 7
8 + 3
4 + 7

3.

12
8 + 2
6 + 6
9 + 2
6 + 7

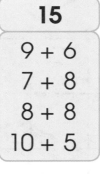

4.

13
8 + 4
6 + 7
4 + 9
10 + 3

5.

14
8 + 6
9 + 5
7 + 7
4 + 10

6.

15
9 + 6
7 + 8
8 + 8
10 + 5

7.

16
8 + 9
10 + 6
9 + 7
8 + 8

8.

17
8 + 8
9 + 8
9 + 9
10 + 7

9.

18
8 + 8
8 + 10
9 + 9
8 + 9

Practice the addition facts.
Write the missing **sums** in the chart.

+	0	1	2	3	4	5	6	7	8	9
0	0			3		5	6		8	
1		2								10
2	2			5				9		
3		4								
4	4			7			10			
5		6								14
6						11				
7	7									
8		9					14			17
9	9			12				16		

Adding Doubles

Learn the **doubles facts** to make adding easier.

Learn these **doubles facts** so you can say them as fast as you can!

1 + 1 = 2	4 + 4 = 8	7 + 7 = 14
2 + 2 = 4	5 + 5 = 10	8 + 8 = 16
3 + 3 = 6	6 + 6 = 12	9 + 9 = 18

Find the **sum**.

1. 3 + 3 = _____   2. 2 + 2 = _____   3. 5 + 5 = _____

4. 1 + 1 = _____   5. 6 + 6 = _____   6. 8 + 8 = _____

7. 4 + 4 = _____   8. 7 + 7 = _____   9. 9 + 9 = _____

10. 6 + 6 = _____   11. 3 + 3 = _____

12. 2 + 2 = _____   13. 4 + 4 = _____

14. 1 + 1 = _____   15. 7 + 7 = _____

Addition Doubles Facts

A **double plus 1 fact** is a double fact and 1 more.

Learn the **doubles plus 1 facts**. They're easy if you know the doubles facts.

$$2 + 2 + 1 = 5 \qquad 2 + 3 = 5$$

Find the **sum**.

1. $4 + 5 = \underline{\hphantom{00}}$ 2. $1 + 2 = \underline{\hphantom{00}}$ 3. $3 + 4 = \underline{\hphantom{00}}$

4. $6 + 7 = \underline{\hphantom{00}}$ 5. $2 + 3 = \underline{\hphantom{00}}$ 6. $8 + 9 = \underline{\hphantom{00}}$

7. $7 + 8 = \underline{\hphantom{00}}$ 8. $3 + 4 = \underline{\hphantom{00}}$ 9. $6 + 7 = \underline{\hphantom{00}}$

10. $8 + 9 = \underline{\hphantom{00}}$ 11. $4 + 5 = \underline{\hphantom{00}}$

12. $1 + 2 = \underline{\hphantom{00}}$ 13. $6 + 7 = \underline{\hphantom{00}}$

14. $2 + 3 = \underline{\hphantom{00}}$ 15. $8 + 9 = \underline{\hphantom{00}}$

Addition Doubles Plus 1 Facts

Find the **sums**.

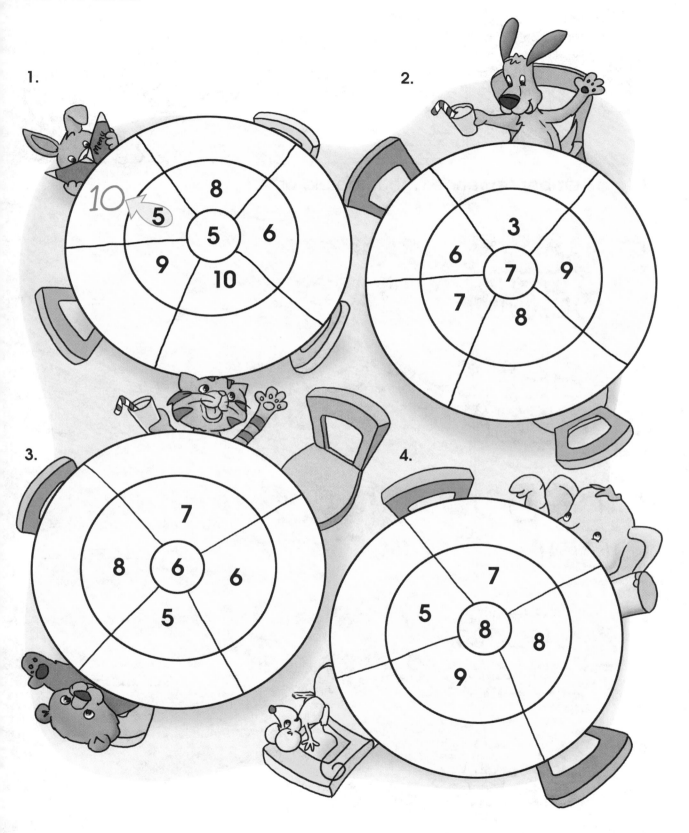

1.

2.

3.

4.

Practicing Addition Facts

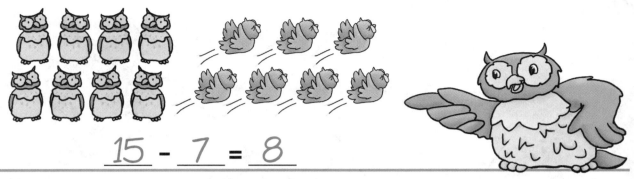

$$\underline{15} - \underline{7} = \underline{8}$$

Write a **number sentence** about the pictures.

1.    _____ − _____ = _____

2.   _____ − _____ = _____

3.   _____ − _____ = _____

4.   _____ − _____ = _____

5.   _____ − _____ = _____

Subtraction Facts to 18

As you've learned, you can use a number line to find **differences**.

$$13 - 7 = 6$$

Find the **difference**. Use the number line if you need help.

1. 14
    $- \ 8$

2. 15
    $- \ 7$

3. 12
    $- \ 4$

4. 15
    $- \ 9$

5. 13
    $- \ 7$

6. 17
    $- \ 8$

7. 14
    $- \ 7$

8. 12
    $- \ 5$

9. 16
    $- \ 9$

10. 13
    $- \ 4$

11. $13 - 8 = $ _____

12. $16 - 8 = $ _____

13. $14 - 9 = $ _____

14. $10 - 7 = $ _____

15. $11 - 5 = $ _____

16. $11 - 3 = $ _____

17. $12 - 9 = $ _____

18. $18 - 9 = $ _____

19. $11 - 7 = $ _____

Subtraction Facts 10–18

Find the missing numbers to complete the **fact family**.

1.

12

$5 + 7 = \boxed{}$

$7 + \boxed{} = 12$

$12 - 5 = \boxed{}$

$12 - 7 = \boxed{}$

2.

13

$\boxed{} + 9 = 13$

$9 + 4 = \boxed{}$

$13 - \boxed{} = 9$

$13 - \boxed{} = 4$

3.

14

$8 + 6 = \boxed{}$

$6 + \boxed{} = 14$

$14 - 8 = \boxed{}$

$14 - 6 = \boxed{}$

4.

15

$8 + \boxed{} = 15$

$7 + 8 = \boxed{}$

$15 - \boxed{} = 7$

$15 - \boxed{} = 8$

5.

16

$\boxed{} + 7 = 16$

$7 + 9 = \boxed{}$

$16 - 9 = \boxed{}$

$16 - 7 = \boxed{}$

6.

17

$8 + \boxed{} = 17$

$9 + 8 = \boxed{}$

$17 - \boxed{} = 9$

$17 - \boxed{} = 8$

Fact Families 12–17

Think of addition doubles facts to find **subtraction doubles facts**.

$12 - 6 = 6$ $6 + 6 = 12$
$12 - 6 = 6$

Think of addition doubles plus 1 facts to find **subtraction doubles plus 1 facts**.

$13 - 6 = 7$ $6 + 6 + 1 = 13$
$13 - 6 = 6 + 1$

Find the **difference**.

1. $\begin{array}{r} 14 \\ -\ 7 \\ \hline \end{array}$
2. $\begin{array}{r} 12 \\ -\ 6 \\ \hline \end{array}$
3. $\begin{array}{r} 10 \\ -\ 5 \\ \hline \end{array}$
4. $\begin{array}{r} 16 \\ -\ 8 \\ \hline \end{array}$
5. $\begin{array}{r} 18 \\ -\ 9 \\ \hline \end{array}$

6. $\begin{array}{r} 15 \\ -\ 7 \\ \hline \end{array}$
7. $\begin{array}{r} 13 \\ -\ 6 \\ \hline \end{array}$
8. $\begin{array}{r} 11 \\ -\ 5 \\ \hline \end{array}$
9. $\begin{array}{r} 17 \\ -\ 8 \\ \hline \end{array}$
10. $\begin{array}{r} 17 \\ -\ 9 \\ \hline \end{array}$

11. $\begin{array}{r} 15 \\ -\ 8 \\ \hline \end{array}$
12. $\begin{array}{r} 13 \\ -\ 7 \\ \hline \end{array}$
13. $\begin{array}{r} 11 \\ -\ 6 \\ \hline \end{array}$

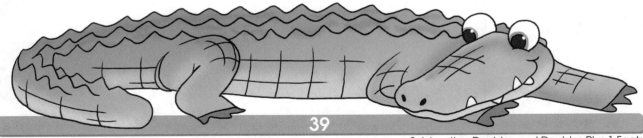

Subtraction Doubles and Doubles Plus 1 Facts

Find the **missing number** in the problem.
Remember the addition and subtraction facts.

1. $7 + 3 = \boxed{}$ 2. $5 + 6 = \boxed{}$ 3. $8 + 9 = \boxed{}$

4. $12 - 8 = \boxed{}$ 5. $18 - 9 = \boxed{}$ 6. $15 - 8 = \boxed{}$

7. $8 + \boxed{} = 9$ 8. $11 - \boxed{} = 2$ 9. $5 + \boxed{} = 14$

10. $13 - 8 = \boxed{}$ 11. $14 - 8 = \boxed{}$ 12. $13 - 7 = \boxed{}$

Write the **sums** or **differences**.

13. Subtract **5**	14. Add **6**	15. Subtract **7**	16. Add **8**
10 _____	8 _____	14 _____	6 _____
13 _____	5 _____	15 _____	8 _____
11 _____	9 _____	11 _____	7 _____
14 _____	7 _____	9 _____	9 _____

Practice Facts 0–18

Write each **sum** and **difference**.
Circle the flamingo with the greatest answer.

1.	2.	3.	4.	5.	6.
8	17	10	15	7	6
+ 7	− 9	− 2	− 6	+ 8	+ 3
− 9	− 5	− 8	+ 4	− 6	+ 5
+ 7	+ 9	+ 7	− 9	+ 9	− 6
=	=	=	=	=	=

Addition and Subtraction Facts 0–18

1. Add the **ones**.   **2.** Add the **tens**.

Tens Ones

```
   5 3
 +   4
 ───────
     7
```

Tens Ones

```
   5 3
 +   4
 ───────
   5 7
```

Add the **ones**.
Then **add** the **tens**.

1.
```
  63
+  4
────
```

2.
```
  91
+  8
────
```

3.
```
  50
+  5
────
```

4.
```
  78
+  1
────
```

5.
```
  25
+  3
────
```

6.
```
  83
+  6
────
```

7.
```
  45
+ 34
────
```

8.
```
  27
+ 70
────
```

9.
```
  44
+ 42
────
```

10.
```
  32
+ 66
────
```

11.
```
  46
+ 53
────
```

12.
```
  37
+ 32
────
```

Adding More Tens and Ones

Solve the riddle.
Remember: **Add** the **ones** and then the **tens**.

Riddle:
What animal can fit an elephant on its tongue?

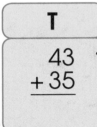

1.
W
$$56 \\ +30$$

2.
C
$$71 \\ +25$$

3.
T
$$43 \\ +35$$

4.
W
$$20 \\ +74$$

5.
A
$$81 \\ +14$$

6.
J
$$90 \\ +\ 7$$

7.
R
$$85 \\ +14$$

8.
G
$$34 \\ +30$$

9.
U
$$20 \\ +61$$

10.
E
$$17 \\ +42$$

11.
H
$$55 \\ +11$$

12.
L
$$62 \\ +\ 6$$

13.
W
$$47 \\ +30$$

14.
L
$$21 \\ +\ 4$$

15.
E
$$40 \\ +30$$

16.
B
$$26 \\ +23$$

The ___ ___ ___ ___ ___ ___ ___ ___ ___
49 25 81 70   94 66 95 68 59

Adding Tens and Ones

1. **Subtract** the **ones.**

Tens	Ones
4	9
−	5
	4

2. **Subtract** the **tens.**

Tens	Ones
4	9
−	5
4	4

Subtract the **ones.**
Then **subtract** the **tens.**

1. 57
   − 2

2. 45
   − 3

3. 69
   − 7

4. 78
   − 5

5. 24
   − 3

6. 98
   − 6

7. 47
   − 22

8. 66
   − 43

9. 89
   − 26

10. 59
   − 23

11. 76
   − 34

12. 99
   − 47

The way
to an

Remember: **Subtract** the **ones** and then the **tens**.

1. 58 − 36	**2.** 77 − 30	**3.** 45 − 24	**4.** 26 − 5

5. 86 − 3	**6.** 38 − 17	**7.** 67 − 21	**8.** 53 − 30

9. 99 − 65	**10.** 85 − 45	**11.** 78 − 4	**12.** 37 − 30

13. 48 − 25	**14.** 59 − 30	**15.** 76 − 24	**16.** 87 − 3

Subtracting Tens and Ones

Find each **sum** and **difference**.
Connect the dots from the **least** number to the **greatest** number.

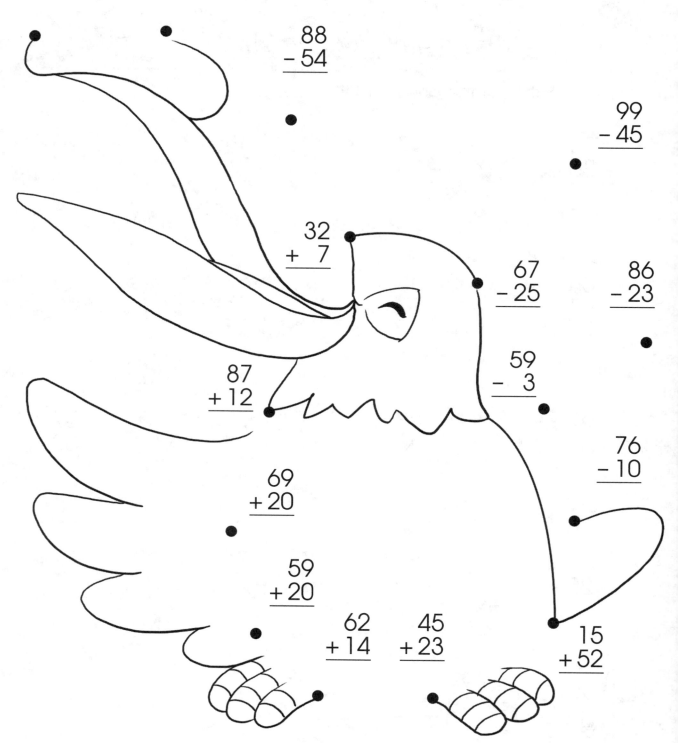

$$\begin{array}{r} 28 \\ -\ 5 \\ \hline \end{array}$$

$$\begin{array}{r} 21 \\ +\ 5 \\ \hline \end{array}$$

$$\begin{array}{r} 44 \\ -\ 3 \\ \hline \end{array}$$

$$\begin{array}{r} 88 \\ -54 \\ \hline \end{array}$$

$$\begin{array}{r} 99 \\ -45 \\ \hline \end{array}$$

$$\begin{array}{r} 32 \\ +\ 7 \\ \hline \end{array}$$

$$\begin{array}{r} 67 \\ -25 \\ \hline \end{array}$$

$$\begin{array}{r} 86 \\ -23 \\ \hline \end{array}$$

$$\begin{array}{r} 87 \\ +12 \\ \hline \end{array}$$

$$\begin{array}{r} 59 \\ -\ 3 \\ \hline \end{array}$$

$$\begin{array}{r} 76 \\ -10 \\ \hline \end{array}$$

$$\begin{array}{r} 69 \\ +20 \\ \hline \end{array}$$

$$\begin{array}{r} 59 \\ +20 \\ \hline \end{array}$$

$$\begin{array}{r} 62 \\ +14 \\ \hline \end{array}$$

$$\begin{array}{r} 45 \\ +23 \\ \hline \end{array}$$

$$\begin{array}{r} 15 \\ +52 \\ \hline \end{array}$$

Help the lion cub find its mother.
Find each **missing number** to finish the
puzzle and get the lion cub home.

$$\begin{array}{r} 3 \\ 1 \\ + 7 \\ \hline \square \end{array}$$

$$\begin{array}{r} 9 \\ 2 \\ + 1 \\ \hline \square \end{array}$$

$$\begin{array}{r} 2 \\ 4 \\ + 5 \\ \hline \square \end{array}$$

$$\begin{array}{r} 50 \\ + 8 \\ \hline \square \end{array}$$

$$\begin{array}{r} 6 \\ - 4 \\ \hline \square \end{array}$$

$$\begin{array}{r} 4 \\ 7 \\ + 1 \\ \hline \square \end{array}$$

$$\begin{array}{r} 44 \\ +34 \\ \hline \square \end{array}$$

$$\begin{array}{r} 5 \\ + \square \\ \hline 8 \end{array}$$

$$\begin{array}{r} 5 \\ 2 \\ + 3 \\ \hline \square \end{array}$$

$$\begin{array}{r} 38 \\ - 5 \\ \hline \square \end{array}$$

$$\begin{array}{r} 29 \\ - 2 \\ \hline \square \end{array}$$

$$\begin{array}{r} 8 \\ + \square \\ \hline 12 \end{array}$$

$$\begin{array}{r} 12 \\ - 7 \\ \hline \square \end{array}$$

$$\begin{array}{r} 69 \\ +20 \\ \hline \square \end{array}$$

$$\begin{array}{r} 7 \\ + \square \\ \hline 11 \end{array}$$

$$\begin{array}{r} 12 \\ - 8 \\ \hline \square \end{array}$$

$$\begin{array}{r} 5 \\ + \square \\ \hline 11 \end{array}$$

$$\begin{array}{r} 59 \\ - 3 \\ \hline \square \end{array}$$

$$\begin{array}{r} 13 \\ + \square \\ \hline 15 \end{array}$$

$$\begin{array}{r} 5 \\ + \square \\ \hline 12 \end{array}$$

1. Add the **ones**.
6 + 6 = 12
Regroup 12 ones
as **1** ten and **2** ones.

Tens Ones
  1
  3 6
+   6
    2

2. Add the **tens**.
3 + 1 = **4** tens

Tens Ones
  1
  3 6
+   6
  4 2

Add. **Regroup** as needed.

1. 58 + 4	**2.** 24 + 7	**3.** 36 + 4	**4.** 75 + 6

5. 48 +34	**6.** 62 +18	**7.** 78 + 7	**8.** 59 +24

9. 67 +18	**10.** 56 +24	**11.** 29 +58	**12.** 45 +35

13. 76 +18	**14.** 54 +27	**15.** 43 +49	**16.** 87 + 8

Add. Regroup as needed.

1. $\begin{array}{r} 59 \\ +7 \\ \hline \end{array}$

2. $\begin{array}{r} 74 \\ +15 \\ \hline \end{array}$

3. $\begin{array}{r} 85 \\ +7 \\ \hline \end{array}$

4. $\begin{array}{r} 76 \\ +12 \\ \hline \end{array}$

5. $\begin{array}{r} 70 \\ +19 \\ \hline \end{array}$

6. $\begin{array}{r} 66 \\ +23 \\ \hline \end{array}$

7. $\begin{array}{r} 48 \\ +23 \\ \hline \end{array}$

8. $\begin{array}{r} 27 \\ +8 \\ \hline \end{array}$

9. $\begin{array}{r} 88 \\ +7 \\ \hline \end{array}$

10. $\begin{array}{r} 40 \\ +28 \\ \hline \end{array}$

11. $\begin{array}{r} 75 \\ +17 \\ \hline \end{array}$

12. $\begin{array}{r} 29 \\ +65 \\ \hline \end{array}$

How many miles can these animals swim in an hour?

Swordfish   Dolphin   Tuna   Sailfish   Sea Turtle

13. $\begin{array}{r} 32 \\ +18 \\ \hline \end{array}$

14. $\begin{array}{r} 16 \\ +9 \\ \hline \end{array}$

15. $\begin{array}{r} 31 \\ +9 \\ \hline \end{array}$

16. $\begin{array}{r} 37 \\ +28 \\ \hline \end{array}$

17. $\begin{array}{r} 12 \\ +8 \\ \hline \end{array}$

_____ miles   _____ miles   _____ miles   _____ miles   _____ miles

1. **Subtract** the **ones**.
4 – 6 cannot be done!
You must **regroup**.

$$\begin{array}{r} 5\ 4 \\ -\ 1\ 6 \\ \hline ? \end{array}$$

2. **Subtract** the **tens**.
4 – 1 = 3 tens

Tens Ones
4 14
$$\begin{array}{r} \cancel{5}\ \cancel{4} \\ -\ 1\ 6 \\ \hline 3\ 8 \end{array}$$

54 is **5** tens and **4** ones.
Regroup as **4** tens and **14** ones.
14 – 6 = 8

Tens Ones
4 14
$$\begin{array}{r} \cancel{5}\ \cancel{4} \\ -\ 1\ 6 \\ \hline 8 \end{array}$$

Subtract. Regroup as needed.

1.
$$\begin{array}{r} 57 \\ -\ 9 \\ \hline \end{array}$$

2.
$$\begin{array}{r} 24 \\ -10 \\ \hline \end{array}$$

3.
$$\begin{array}{r} 36 \\ -17 \\ \hline \end{array}$$

4.
$$\begin{array}{r} 82 \\ -66 \\ \hline \end{array}$$

5.
$$\begin{array}{r} 75 \\ -23 \\ \hline \end{array}$$

6.
$$\begin{array}{r} 43 \\ -18 \\ \hline \end{array}$$

7.
$$\begin{array}{r} 61 \\ -56 \\ \hline \end{array}$$

8.
$$\begin{array}{r} 40 \\ -27 \\ \hline \end{array}$$

9.
$$\begin{array}{r} 94 \\ -58 \\ \hline \end{array}$$

10.
$$\begin{array}{r} 38 \\ -\ 9 \\ \hline \end{array}$$

11.
$$\begin{array}{r} 88 \\ -78 \\ \hline \end{array}$$

12.
$$\begin{array}{r} 55 \\ -27 \\ \hline \end{array}$$

13.
$$\begin{array}{r} 18 \\ -\ 6 \\ \hline \end{array}$$

14.
$$\begin{array}{r} 44 \\ -17 \\ \hline \end{array}$$

15.
$$\begin{array}{r} 70 \\ -35 \\ \hline \end{array}$$

16.
$$\begin{array}{r} 39 \\ -19 \\ \hline \end{array}$$

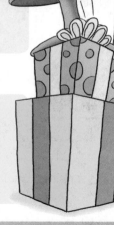

Subtracting Tens and Ones with Regrouping

Subtract. Regroup as needed.

1. 54
    − 7

2. 67
    − 8

3. 82
    − 5

4. 40
    − 6

5. 22
    − 4

6. 95
    − 7

7. 73
    − 8

8. 36
    − 7

9. 48
    − 29

10. 50
    − 25

11. 26
    − 17

12. 34
    − 25

Which animal is the longest? Circle the answer.

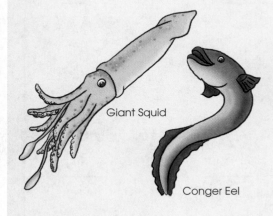

Giant Squid

Conger Eel

Flying Fish

Whale Shark

Atlantic Manta

13. 85
    − 45

    _____ feet

14. 36
    − 27

    _____ feet

15. 30
    − 29

    _____ foot

16. 74
    − 19

    _____ feet

17. 76
    − 58

    _____ feet

Find the **sum** or **difference**. **Regroup** as needed.

1. 45
   +35

2. 89
   −62

3. 36
   −18

4. 72
   +18

5. 50
   −25

6. 65
   +28

7. 91
   + 8

8. 25
   +25

9. 32
   +48

10. 49
    +37

11. 74
    −28

12. 19
    −17

13. 88
    −66

14. 36
    +36

15. 67
    −18

16. 91
    −19

Adding and Subtracting Tens and Ones with Regrouping

©School Zone Publishing Company

Find the **sum** or **difference**.
Regroup as needed.
Write the answers in the puzzle.

Down

1.
$$60 - 35$$

3.
$$28 + 19$$

4.
$$25 + 28$$

5.
$$66 - 29$$

9.
$$43 + 50$$

10.
$$53 + 17$$

11.
$$47 + 16$$

Across

1.
$$53 - 26$$

2.
$$35 + 49$$

4.
$$75 - 70$$

6.
$$72 - 65$$

7.
$$45 + 32$$

8.
$$90 - 86$$

10.
$$36 + 36$$

12.
$$86 - 49$$

13.
$$56 - 23$$

Adding and Subtracting Tens and Ones with Regrouping

Adding without regrouping:

1. **Add** the **ones**.
   4 + 3 = **7** ones

2. **Add** the **tens**.
   3 + 5 = **8** tens

3. **Add** the **hundreds**.
   5 + 2 = **7** hundreds

```
  Hundreds Tens Ones
    5    3    4
 +  2    5    3
 ─────────────
    7    8    7
```

Adding with regrouping:

1. **Add** the **ones**.
   7 + 5 = **12** ones
   Regroup 12 ones as
   1 ten and **2** ones.

2. **Add** the **tens**.
   1 + 2 + 5 = **8** tens

3. **Add** the **hundreds**.
   6 + 1 = **7** hundreds

```
  Hundreds Tens Ones
           1
    6    2    7
 +  1    5    5
 ─────────────
    7    8    2
```

Add. Regroup as needed.

1. 547
   + 345

2. 136
   + 546

3. 481
   + 209

4. 628
   + 167

5. 287
   + 707

6. 345
   + 248

7. 407
   + 486

8. 524
   + 127

9. 753
   + 118

Adding Three-Digit Numbers with Regrouping

When adding greater numbers, you may have to **regroup** more than once.

1. **Add** the **ones**.
   8 + 5 = **13** ones
   Regroup **13** ones as **1** ten and **3** ones.

2. **Add** the **tens**.
   1 + 6 + 7 = **14** tens
   Regroup **14** tens as
   1 hundred and **4** tens.

3. **Add** the **hundreds**.
   1 + 5 + 2 = **8** hundreds

Hundreds	Tens	Ones
1	1	
5	**6**	**8**
+2	**7**	**5**
8	**4**	**3**

Add. Regroup as needed.

1. 584
   + 372

2. 240
   + 495

3. 798
   + 114

4. 591
   + 147

5. 278
   + 243

6. 632
   + 287

7. 745
   + 187

8. 188
   + 181

9. 276
   + 575

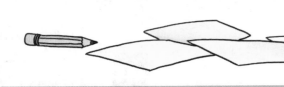

55

Adding Three-Digit Numbers with Regrouping

1. **Subtract** the **ones**.
   5 – 8 cannot be done!
   Regroup 7 tens **5** ones
   as **6** tens **15** ones.
   15 – 8 = 7 ones

2. **Subtract** the **tens**.
   6 – 2 = 4 tens

3. **Subtract** the **hundreds**.
   5 – 2 = 3 hundreds

```
  Hundreds Tens Ones
          6  15
     5  7  5
  -  2  2  8
  ─────────────
     3  4  7
```

Subtract. Regroup as needed.

1.   574
   − 458

2.   356
   − 149

3.   825
   − 207

4.   756
   − 348

5.   473
   − 158

6.   392
   − 347

7.   864
   − 508

8.   615
   − 208

9.   973
   − 755

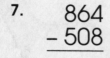

Subtracting Three-Digit Numbers with Regrouping

Find the **sum** or **difference**. **Regroup** as needed.

1.
```
  585
- 269
```

2.
```
  274
+ 234
```

3.
```
  108
+ 544
```

4.
```
  922
- 108
```

5.
```
  184
+ 507
```

6.
```
  355
- 118
```

7.
```
  571
+ 262
```

8.
```
  963
- 125
```

9.
```
  456
+ 138
```

10.
```
  222
- 115
```

11.
```
  753
+ 156
```

12.
```
  151
- 138
```

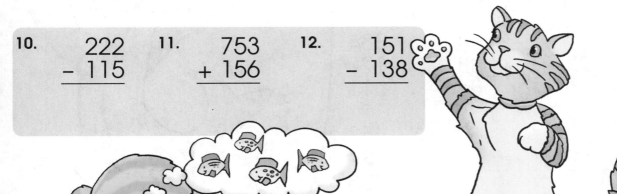

Adding and Subtracting Three-Digit Numbers with Regrouping

Cross out the incorrect answers.
Write the correct answers.
Which seal has the most correct answers? _____

Sid

```
  64        36        387
+ 23      + 27      +116
  97        63        493

  84        73        460
- 36      - 27      -129
  98        46        342
```

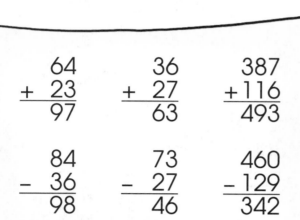

Sammy

```
  39        47        392
+ 25      + 35      +138
  64        82        530

  79        83        467
- 34      - 36      -138
  35        47        329
```

```
  39        44        384
+ 27      + 38      +127
  66        86        511

  88        60        452
- 39      - 27      -137
  49        33        325
```

Sally

Adding and Subtracting Two-Digit and Three-Digit Numbers with Regrouping   ©School Zone Publishing Company

Recall basic facts.

1. 9 + 5 = _____   **2.** 6 + 0 = _____   **3.** 7 + 9 = _____   **4.** 4 + 7 = _____

5. 17 − 8 = _____   **6.** 13 − 5 = _____   **7.** 15 − 9 = _____   **8.** 10 − 4 = _____

9. 8 + 8 = _____   **10.** 14 − 6 = _____   **11.** 9 + 9 = _____   **12.** 11 − 2 = _____

Add. Find the **sum. Regroup** as needed.

13.	14.	15.	16.
43 +25	50 +30	74 + 5	26 +52

17.	18.	19.	20.
38 +25	57 + 9	66 +17	28 +32

Subtract. Find the **difference. Regroup** as needed.

21.	22.	23.	24.
76 − 45	93 − 40	59 − 29	27 − 7

25.	26.	27.	28.
35 − 7	54 − 29	75 − 68	60 − 24

Add or **subtract. Regroup** as needed.

29.	30.	31.	32.
342 +236	536 +125	456 − 327	745 − 129

Review

Answer Key

Page 1
1. $2 + 2 = 4$
2. $3 + 3 = 6$
3. $4 + 2 = 6$
4. $1 + 3 = 4$
5. $1 + 1 = 2$
6. $5 + 1 = 6$
7. $2 + 3 = 5$

Page 2
1. 6
2. 5
3. 6
4. 6
5. 5
6. 4
7. 5
8. 6
9. 6
10. 2
11. 6
12. 4
13. 3
14. 6
15. 5
16. 4

Page 3
1. $4 - 3 = 1$
2. $6 - 3 = 3$
3. $2 - 1 = 1$
4. $5 - 2 = 3$
5. $4 - 2 = 2$
6. $6 - 4 = 2$
7. $6 - 1 = 5$

Page 4
1. 3
2. 3
3. 2
4. 1
5. 2
6. 1
7. 4
8. 2
9. 2
10. 5
11. 1
12. 2
13. 3
14. 1
15. 3
16. 1
17. 1
18. 4

Page 5
1. 4
2. 3
3. 6
4. 5
5. 2
6. 2
7. 5
8. 1
9. 4
10. 6
11. 2
12. 1
13. 3
14. 3
15. 0
16. 5
17. 5
18. 0
19. 2
20. 4

Page 6
1. 4, 4, 3, 1
2. 6, 6, 1, 5
3. 4, 4, 0, 4
4. 6, 3
5. 6, 3
6. 4, 2

Page 7
1. 5, 3, 1, 6
2. 4, 6, 5, 3
3. 6, 4, 1, 5
4. 5, 2, 4, 1
5. 5, 2, 6, 1
6. 0, 1, 4, 3
7. $\boxed{2} +4 \boxed{6} -3 \boxed{3} -1 \boxed{2} +2 = \boxed{4}$ 🐞s

Page 8
1. $3 + 4 = 7$
2. $5 + 2 = 7$
3. $1 + 6 = 7$
4. $5 + 3 = 8$
5. $7 + 1 = 8$
6. $2 + 6 = 8$
7. $4 + 4 = 8$

Page 9
1. $7 - 5 = 2$
2. $7 - 4 = 3$
3. $7 - 1 = 6$
4. $7 - 3 = 4$
5. $8 - 5 = 3$
6. $7 - 0 = 7$
7. $8 - 7 = 1$

Page 10
1. 7
2. 8
3. 4
4. 5
5. 7
6. 3
7. 7
8. 8
9. 6
10. 8
11. 5
12. 7
13. 6
14. 3
15. 2
16. 5
17. 8
18. 4
19. 8

Page 11
1. 7, 7, 3, 4
2. 8, 4
3. 7, 7, 5, 2
4. 8, 8, 6, 2
5. 8, 8, 1, 7
6. 8, 0

Page 12
1. $4 + 5 = 9$
2. $2 + 7 = 9$
3. $3 + 7 = 10$
4. $8 + 2 = 10$
5. $3 + 6 = 9$
6. $4 + 6 = 10$
7. $5 + 5 = 10$

Page 13
1. $9 - 4 = 5$
2. $9 - 2 = 7$
3. $9 - 6 = 3$
4. $10 - 8 = 2$
5. $10 - 4 = 6$
6. $10 - 7 = 3$
7. $10 - 5 = 5$

Page 14
1. 9, 9, 3, 6
2. 9, 9, 4, 5
3. 10, 10, 4, 6
4. 10, 10, 3, 7
5. 10, 10, 8, 2
6. 5, 10

Page 15
1. 6
2. 9
3. 5
4. 10
5. 2
6. 8
7. 10
8. 6
9. 9
10. 10
11. 10
12. 9
13. 3
14. 7
15. 10
16. 10
17. 5
18. 8

Page 16
1. 6
2. 3
3. 10
4. 10
5. 8
6. 8
7. 3
8. 9
9. 4
10. 9
11. 3
12. 7
13. 6
14. 7
15. 7
16. 2
17. 8
18. 10
19. 6
20. 9

Answer Key

Page 17
1. + 2. – 3. – 4. +
5. – 6. + 7. – 8. –
9. + 10. – 11. – 12. +
13. + 14. – 15. – 16. +

Page 18
1. 3 + 8 = 11
2. 9 + 2 = 11
3. 3 + 9 = 12
4. 5 + 7 = 12
5. 6 + 6 = 12
6. 7 + 4 = 11

Page 19
1. 11 2. 12 3. 10
4. 11 5. 9 6. 9
7. 11 8. 9 9. 10
10. 12 11. 10 12. 11 13. 12
14. 12 15. 10 16. 9 17. 10
18. 10 19. 12 20. 9 21. 11

Page 20
1. 12 – 3 = 9
2. 11 – 6 = 5
3. 12 – 6 = 6
4. 11 – 8 = 3
5. 11 – 2 = 9
6. 12 – 5 = 7

Page 21
1. 8 2. 3 3. 4
4. 8 5. 5 6. 9
7. 3 8. 4 9. 9
10. 3 11. 6 12. 2 13. 1
14. 7 15. 5 16. 3 17. 6
18. 3 19. 5 20. 7 21. 9

Page 22
1. 11, 11, 9, 2 2. 12, 6
3. 12, 12, 8, 4 4. 11, 11, 6, 5
5. 11, 11, 7, 4 6. 11, 11, 8, 3
7. 12, 12, 3, 9 8. 12, 12, 7, 5

Page 23

1.	2.	3.	4.	5.	6.
9	4	12	0	7	5
+ 3	+ 7	– 8	+ 9	– 3	+ 2
12	11	4	9	4	7
– 6	– 6	– 4	+ 2	+ 8	– 4
6	5	0	11	12	3
– 3	+ 5	+ 5	– 7	– 4	– 2
=	=	=	=	=	=
3	10	5	4	8	1

Page 24
1. 11 2. 12 3. 12 4. 11
5. 12 6. 10 7. 11 8. 12
9. 10 10. 12 11. 10 12. 11

Page 26
1. 4 + 9 = 13
2. 6 + 7 = 13
3. 7 + 7 = 14
4. 8 + 5 = 13
5. 8 + 6 = 14
6. 9 + 5 = 14

Page 25

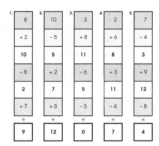

1.	2.	3.	4.	5.
8	10	3	2	7
+ 2	– 5	+ 8	+ 6	– 4
10	5	11	8	3
– 8	+ 2	– 6	+ 3	+ 9
2	7	5	11	12
+ 7	+ 5	– 5	– 4	– 8
=	=	=	=	=
9	12	0	7	4
L	I	O	N	S

Page 29
1. 12 2. 7 3. 5
4. 6 5. 8 6. 14
7. 4 8. 13 9. 5
10. 11 11. 8 12. 12 13. 8 14. 4
15. 8 16. 6 17. 12 18. 8 19. 8

Page 27
1. 11 2. 11 3. 14 4. 14
5. 11 6. 11 7. 10 8. 10
9. 13 10. 13 11. 13 12. 13
13. 10 14. 10 15. 12 16. 12
17. 13 18. 13 19. 14 20. 14
21. 12 22. 12 23. 11 24. 11
25. 12 26. 12 27. 9 28. 9

Page 28
1. 14 – 8 = 6
2. 13 – 5 = 8
3. 14 – 7 = 7
4. 14 – 5 = 9
5. 13 – 7 = 6
6. 14 – 6 = 8

Page 30
1. 7 + 8 = 15
2. 9 + 9 = 18
3. 8 + 8 = 16
4. 9 + 7 = 16
5. 8 + 9 = 17

Page 31
1. **10**
5 + 5
4 + 6
3 + 8
5 + 4

2. **11**
5 + 6
3 + 7
8 + 3
4 + 7

3. **12**
8 + 2
6 + 6
9 + 2
6 + 7

4. **13**
8 + 4
6 + 7
7 + 7
10 + 3

5. **14**
8 + 6
9 + 5
7 + 7
4 + 10

6. **15**
9 + 6
7 + 8
8 + 8
10 + 5

7. **16**
8 + 9
10 + 6
9 + 7
8 + 8

8. **17**
8 + 8
9 + 8
9 + 9
10 + 7

9. **18**
8 + 8
8 + 10
9 + 9
8 + 9

Page 32

+	0	1	2	3	4	5	6	7	8	9
0	0	1	2	3	4	5	6	7	8	9
1	1	2	3	4	5	6	7	8	9	10
2	2	3	4	5	6	7	8	9	10	11
3	3	4	5	6	7	8	9	10	11	12
4	4	5	6	7	8	9	10	11	12	13
5	5	6	7	8	9	10	11	12	13	14
6	6	7	8	9	10	11	12	13	14	15
7	7	8	9	10	11	12	13	14	15	16
8	8	9	10	11	12	13	14	15	16	17
9	9	10	11	12	13	14	15	16	17	18

Answer Key

Answer Key

Page 33
1. 6   2. 4   3. 10
4. 2   5. 12   6. 16
7. 8   8. 14   9. 18
10. 12   11. 6
12. 4   13. 8
14. 2   15. 14

Page 34
1. 9   2. 3   3. 7
4. 13   5. 5   6. 17
7. 15   8. 7   9. 13
10. 17   11. 9
12. 3   13. 13
14. 5   15. 17

Page 35

Page 36
1. 16 – 8 = 8
2. 17 – 8 = 9
3. 15 – 9 = 6
4. 18 – 9 = 9
5. 16 – 7 = 9

Page 37
1. 6   2. 8   3. 8   4. 6   5. 6
6. 9   7. 7   8. 7   9. 7   10. 9
11. 5   12. 8   13. 5
14. 3   15. 6
16. 8   17. 3
18. 9   19. 4

Page 38
1. 12
5 + 7 = 12
7 + 5 = 12
12 – 5 = 7
12 – 7 = 5

2. 13
4 + 9 = 13
9 + 4 = 13
13 – 4 = 9
13 – 9 = 4

3. 14
8 + 6 = 14
6 + 8 = 14
14 – 8 = 6
14 – 6 = 8

4. 15
8 + 7 = 15
7 + 8 = 15
15 – 8 = 7
15 – 7 = 8

5. 16
9 + 7 = 16
7 + 9 = 16
16 – 9 = 7
16 – 7 = 9

6. 17
8 + 9 = 17
9 + 8 = 17
17 – 8 = 9
17 – 9 = 8

Page 39
1. 7   2. 6   3. 5   4. 8   5. 9
6. 8   7. 7   8. 6   9. 9   10. 8
11. 7   12. 6   13. 5

Page 40
1. 10   2. 11   3. 17
4. 4   5. 9   6. 7
7. 1   8. 9   9. 9
10. 5   11. 6   12. 6
13. 5   14. 14   15. 7   16. 14
8   11   8   16
6   15   4   15
9   13   2   17

Page 41

	1.	2.	3.	4.	5.	6.
	8	17	10	15	7	6
	+7	–9	–2	–6	+8	+3
	15	8	8	9	15	9
	–9	–5	–8	+4	–6	+5
	6	3	0	13	9	14
	+7	+9	+7	–9	+9	–6
	=	=	=	=	=	=
	13	12	7	4	18	8

Page 42
1. 67   2. 99   3. 55
4. 79   5. 28   6. 89
7. 79   8. 97   9. 86
10. 98   11. 99   12. 69

Page 43
1. 86   2. 96   3. 78   4. 94
5. 95   6. 97   7. 99   8. 64
9. 81   10. 59   11. 66   12. 68
13. 77   14. 25   15. 70   16. 49
The BLUE WHALE

Page 44
1. 55   2. 42   3. 62
4. 73   5. 21   6. 92
7. 25   8. 23   9. 63
10. 36   11. 42   12. 52

Page 45
1. 22   2. 47   3. 21   4. 21
5. 83   6. 21   7. 46   8. 23
9. 34   10. 40   11. 74   12. 7
13. 23   14. 29   15. 52   16. 84

Page 46

Answer Key

Page 47

Page 48

1. 62	**2.** 31	**3.** 40	**4.** 81
5. 82	**6.** 80	**7.** 85	**8.** 83
9. 85	**10.** 80	**11.** 87	**12.** 80
13. 94	**14.** 81	**15.** 92	**16.** 95

Page 49

1. 66	**2.** 89	**3.** 92	**4.** 88	
5. 89	**6.** 89	**7.** 71	**8.** 35	
9. 95	**10.** 68	**11.** 92	**12.** 94	
13. 50	**14.** 25	**15.** 40	**16.** 65	**17.** 20

Page 50

1. 48	**2.** 14	**3.** 19	**4.** 16
5. 52	**6.** 25	**7.** 5	**8.** 13
9. 36	**10.** 29	**11.** 10	**12.** 28
13. 12	**14.** 27	**15.** 35	**16.** 20

Page 51

1. 47	**2.** 59	**3.** 77	**4.** 34	
5. 18	**6.** 88	**7.** 65	**8.** 29	
9. 19	**10.** 25	**11.** 9	**12.** 9	
13. 40	**14.** 9	**15.** 1	**16.** 55	**17.** 18

Page 52

1. 80	**2.** 27	**3.** 18	**4.** 90
5. 25	**6.** 93	**7.** 99	**8.** 50
9. 80	**10.** 86	**11.** 46	**12.** 2
13. 22	**14.** 72	**15.** 49	**16.** 72

Page 53

¹2	7		²8	4	⁴5
5		⁵3		⁷7	3
	⁷7	7		⁸4	
⁹9		¹⁰	7	2	¹¹6
¹²3	7		0	¹³3	3

Page 54

1. 892	**2.** 682	**3.** 690
4. 795	**5.** 994	**6.** 593
7. 893	**8.** 651	**9.** 871

Page 55

1. 956	**2.** 735	**3.** 912
4. 738	**5.** 521	**6.** 919
7. 932	**8.** 369	**9.** 851

Page 56

1. 116	**2.** 207	**3.** 618
4. 408	**5.** 315	**6.** 45
7. 356	**8.** 407	**9.** 218

Page 57

1. 316	**2.** 508	**3.** 652
4. 814	**5.** 691	**6.** 237
7. 833	**8.** 838	**9.** 594
10. 107	**11.** 909	**12.** 13

Page 58

Sally has the most correct answers.

Page 59

1. 14	**2.** 6	**3.** 16	**4.** 11
5. 9	**6.** 8	**7.** 6	**8.** 6
9. 16	**10.** 8	**11.** 18	**12.** 9
13. 68	**14.** 80	**15.** 79	**16.** 78
17. 63	**18.** 66	**19.** 83	**20.** 60
21. 31	**22.** 53	**23.** 30	**24.** 20
25. 28	**26.** 25	**27.** 7	**28.** 36
29. 578	**30.** 661	**31.** 129	**32.** 616

Answer Key

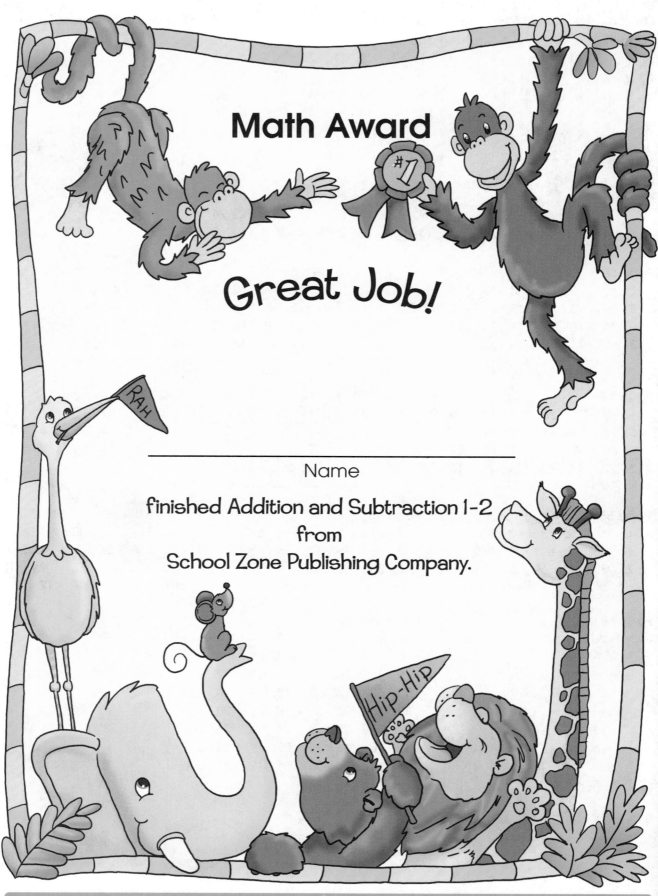

Math Award

Great Job!

_____
Name

finished Addition and Subtraction 1-2
from
School Zone Publishing Company.

Addition & Subtraction 1-2 **02209**